Title Information:	
Date:	
Logbook #:	
Continued from Logbook #:	
Name:	
Title:	
Address:	
City & State:	
Email address:	
Telephone #:	
Date Logbook Started	
Date Logbook Ended	
Signature	

Notes:-

TABLE OF CONTENTS

DATE	SUBJECT	PAGE#

TABLE OF CONTENTS

DATE	SUBJECT	PAGE#

TABLE OF CONTENTS

DATE	SUBJECT	PAGE#

Date:

___/___/___

Date:

___/___/___

Made in the USA
Monee, IL
17 December 2024

74006099R00069